P9-DJA-516

DIFFERENT LIKE ME

A Book For Teens Who Worry
About Their Parents Use Of Alcohol/Drugs

by Evelyn Leite and Pamela Espeland

Johnson Institute Books
Minneapolis 1987

Published by Johnson Institute Books, 7151 Metro Blvd., Minneapolis, MN 55439

Library of Congress Cataloging in Publication Data

Leite, Evelyn.
    Different like me.

    Summary: Suggestions and advice for teens with
alcohol or drug dependent parents.
    1. Children of alcoholic parents—Juvenile
literature.   2. Alcoholics—Family relationships—
Juvenile literature.   3. Alcoholism—Juvenile
literature.   [1. Alcoholism.   2. Drug abuse]
I. Espeland, Pamela, 1951-   II. Title.
HV5132.L45   1986   362.2'92   86-33818
ISBN 0-935908-34-X

PRINTED IN THE UNITED STATES OF AMERICA

10 9 8 7 6 5 4

Cover Design and Illustration: MacLean & Tuminelly
Text Illustrations: Caroline Price

DEDICATION

To Lonny, Robert, Scott, Virginia, Jeff, Vicki, Jay, Susan, Rene, Tracy, Edith, Tony, Wendy, Jerry, Todd, Tim, Amy, Willie, and Paula. You are all very special people who deserve the best life has to offer.

"Jesus loves me this I know"
I learned that song a long time ago.
I forgot it for awhile.
And I forgot how to smile.
The pain of living was so intense,
Nothing in life made any sense.
I wanted to live, I wanted to die,
I hurt so bad, I couldn't cry.
I felt so mad I wanted to spit,
and scream and cry and hit and hit.
The pain so deep, so quiet lay,
I couldn't leave, I couldn't stay.
Thanks to love, I learned what to do.
And thanks to love,
so can you.

— E.L.

To the members of all our families. And especially to Roger, the recovering father of my son.

— P.L.E.

ACKNOWLEDGMENTS

Many thanks to Meryl Tullis, a wonderful woman who taught me how to turn fear into surrender and despair into gratitude.

E.L.

Thanks also to Carole, who brought us together so this book could be done.

P.L.E.

CONTENTS

A FEW WORDS ABOUT "ALCOHOL/DRUGS"

You'll notice that we use the strange-looking word *alcohol/drugs* in the title of this book and in many other places throughout it.

We use it to emphasize that *alcohol is a drug* — just like cocaine, marijuana, uppers, downers, or any other mood-altering substance. Too often people talk about "alcohol and drugs" or "alcohol or drugs," as if alcohol is somehow different from drugs and off by itself. Wrong! Repeat: *Alcohol is a drug.*

If you didn't know that until now, you're not alone. Our culture, our government, even our laws treat alcohol differently than they treat so-called "other drugs" like pot, crack, smack, and so on down the list. As long as you're old enough, you can buy and use alcohol without a prescription. You can get it in a store, a restaurant, or a bar without doing anything illegal. You can give it to your friends (as long as they're old enough). You can even get a license to sell it.

The words *chemical dependence* are often used to describe the condition of being dependent — hooked — on alcohol/drugs. Some people prefer them to words like "addict," "drunk," "junkie," or "alcoholic," maybe because they sound more scientific or polite. We use them here because they're easier and shorter than saying "alcoholism or dependence on other drugs."

In the end, though, it doesn't really matter which words you use. A chemical is a chemical. An addiction is an addiction. A disease is a disease. And pain is pain.

INTRODUCTION

Does someone you love drink too much? Are you starting to think that there's an alcohol/drug problem at your house? And every time this thought crosses your mind, do you tell yourself *NO, it couldn't be — not MY mom (or dad)*?

Even though you may deny it, deep down inside you want to know the truth. Everyone wants to know the truth. Because the longer we live without it, the harder it is to live.

Here's a short quiz that can help you to come closer to the truth. Take a few moments to read the statements and consider whether they fit for you. Each one that does gets a "yes"; each one that doesn't gets a "no."

1. I feel like I get blamed for everything that goes wrong at my house.
   ☐ YES   ☐ NO

2. I feel like I take care of everyone and no one takes care of me.
   ☐ YES   ☐ NO

3. I often feel afraid when people get angry with me.
   ☐ YES   ☐ NO

4. I often feel guilty even when I haven't done anything wrong.
   ☐ YES   ☐ NO

5. I worry about my parents' drinking/using.
   ☐ YES   ☐ NO

6. I sometimes pour out bottles of alcohol I find around the house (or add water to them to dilute them).
   ☐ YES   ☐ NO

7. I daydream almost all the time.
   ☐ YES   ☐ NO

8. I often feel depressed and sad for no apparent reason.
   ☐ YES   ☐ NO

9. I lie about my parents' drinking/using.
   ☐ YES   ☐ NO

10. I try hard to do everything right.
    ☐ YES   ☐ NO

11. I often feel lonely and rejected.
    ☐ YES   ☐ NO

12. I have found alcohol/drugs that my parents have hidden.
    ☐ YES   ☐ NO

13. I often have trouble concentrating, so my schoolwork suffers.
    ☐ YES   ☐ NO

14. I'm afraid to ride in the car with my parents when they've been drinking/using.
    ☐ YES   ☐ NO

15. I feel guilty about my parents' drinking/using — as if it's somehow MY fault.
    ☐ YES   ☐ NO

16. I try to hide the fact that my family seems different from other people's families.
    ☐ YES   ☐ NO

17. I make excuses for my parents when they've been drinking/using.
    ☐ YES   ☐ NO

18. Sometimes I just want to give up.
    ☐ YES   ☐ NO

19. I sometimes get embarrassed by my parents' behavior, especially when they've been drinking/using.
    ☐ YES   ☐ NO

20. I worry a lot and have trouble sleeping.
    ☐ YES   ☐ NO

21. I sometimes feel ashamed of my family.
    ☐ YES   ☐ NO

22. I hate holidays because my parents always get drunk/high.
    ☐ YES   ☐ NO

23. I don't believe the promises my parents make to me.
    ☐ YES   ☐ NO

24. It scares me to be around my parents when they've been drinking/using.
    ☐ YES   ☐ NO

25. I WANT THINGS TO CHANGE!
    ☐ YES   ☐ NO

Did you end up with more yesses than nos? Then you have reason to think that something is wrong at your house. And if one (or both) of your parents drinks a lot or uses other drugs, that something may be a drinking or drug problem.

Most people, when they first say the words "alcoholic" or "addict" or "chemically dependent," spit them out as if they taste bad. (Say them to yourself to see how they taste to you.) Naturally, no one — absolutely *no one* — wants to use these words to describe their own parents.

It might surprise you to learn that there are worse things in life than having a chemically dependent parent. There are worse things in life than feeling the way you feel right now (even though you might not be able to think of anything). The *very worst thing* is to have a chemically dependent parent and refuse to consider it, refuse to admit it, refuse to accept it. The very worst thing is to deny that a problem exists.

Why? Because as long as you keep denying it, you'll spend your whole life believing that there's something wrong with *you*. Every move you make to find out the truth, every thought you think along those lines, will seem like a betrayal of your family.

Chemical dependence is a disease of the mind, the body, and the spirit. It acts like a contagious disease in that it affects not only the chemical dependent but also anyone who lives or works closely with him or her. This means that if your parents are chemically dependent, *their* disease is affecting *you*.

No wonder you feel rotten so much of the time. No wonder you feel afraid and lonely and confused and rejected and sad so much of the time.

The good news is, *you can feel better*. Inside yourself. About yourself.

If you want to feel better, if you *dare* to feel better, this book is for you.

WHAT THIS BOOK IS ABOUT

Different Like Me is a book about how it feels to live with parents who abuse alcohol/drugs. It's also a book about chemical dependence — what it is and what it does to people. In it you'll find answers to questions you may have asked, questions you may have wanted to ask, and questions you may have been afraid to ask.

Recognizing, admitting, and putting words to your feelings is the first step on the road to feeling better. Asking questions is the second step. Getting answers is the third step. Doing something with those answers is the fourth step. And on and on. It's a long road, but walking down it gets easier the further along you go. Guaranteed.

There's something strange going on at our house. Not all the time . . . some days are good and on those days I try to forget what happened on the days that weren't so good.

I try to forget about things. I try to look the other way when things don't look right to me. I'm learning how to live with what's going on — but still I wonder if it really has to be like this.

Nobody understands what I'm going through.

IF YOU ARE LIVING WITH ONE OR MORE CHEMICALLY DEPENDENT PARENTS, YOU ARE NOT ALONE

Fact: Approximately 6 million kids under 18 are growing up in homes where one or both parents abuse alcohol/drugs.

You're part of a BIG crowd. That may not help you feel better, but it should help you feel less isolated and different from everyone else.

Fact: In a typical classroom of 25 students, somewhere between 4 and 6 of them are the children of alcoholic parents.

This means that *someone you know* understands *exactly* what you're going through. Because he or she is going through it, too.

Someone you know has one or more chemically dependent parents.

Someone you know is feeling as confused, guilty, scared, embarrassed, angry, and ashamed as you are.

Our family doesn't seem "normal" — like other families. Yet it's a lot like Barney's family down the block or Connie's family across town. So we must be "normal." . . . Why doesn't it feel that way? Why does my family feel different from everyone else's? Why do I feel different from my friends?

IF YOU ARE LIVING WITH ONE OR MORE CHEMICALLY DEPENDENT PARENTS, YOUR FAMILY IS SPECIAL

Chemically dependent people put alcohol/drugs above everything else in their lives. Not because they *want to*, but because they *have to*.

This makes your family special.

Chemically dependent people drink to get drunk or abuse other drugs to get high. Not because it makes them *feel good*, but because it makes them feel *less bad*.

This makes your family special.

Chemically dependent homes are scenes of secrecy, despair, turmoil, hidden emotions, lies, broken promises, and shattered dreams. They are also scenes of laughter and good times — sometimes. The trouble is, you never know what to expect! So people learn not to trust one another or count on one another.

This makes your family special.

Not necessarily "normal" — but *special*.

I used to laugh when my Dad got drunk and tease him about having a little too much. I used to tiptoe around his hangovers and feel sorry for him when he got that shamefaced look in the morning after drinking a lot the night before. I used to have sympathy for him and I wanted to protect him from Mother's nagging and bring him aspirin for his headaches. I even hung around for hours just in case he needed me.

But now I just feel sad or mad and try to ignore him. Sometimes I even get sick of him and wish he'd go away and stay away and then I feel guilty . . . and when I feel guilty about not liking him I break my neck to be good to him because I don't really want him to go away, I just want him to stop drinking.

YOU MAY NOT BELIEVE THIS AT FIRST, BUT IT'S TRUE...

Chemical dependence is a disease.

People who abuse alcohol/drugs are sick. The trouble is, they don't know it, won't admit it, and usually won't get help for it.

Instead, they will deny that they're sick. They may even blame *you* for their problem.

Have you ever heard your Mom or Dad say, "If it weren't for you, I wouldn't have to drink?" Or "If you had come home on time, I wouldn't have gotten high?" Or "If I didn't have to worry about you, I wouldn't need pills to relax?"

Don't buy it! That's like saying, "If you had done better on your math test, I wouldn't have caught this cold!"

It's silly. It's sad. And it simply isn't so.

When Mom stays out late at night I let her sleep in the next morning and try to stay out of her way. I pretend not to notice when she drags around the house red-eyed, drinking a lot of water or pop or coffee or orange juice. I pretend not to notice that she's in a foul mood or else so nicey-nice that I end up getting away with everything and wonder if she even notices . . . or if she even cares. . . . If I get in her way she finds things for me to do or yells at me or wants to give me a big gooey hug or all those things at once.

HOW DO WE KNOW THAT CHEMICAL DEPENDENCE IS A DISEASE?

The American Medical Association has called it one since 1956.

■ Like any other disease, chemical dependence has symptoms.

People with the flu run a fever and throw up. People with the chicken pox have red spots on their bodies. People with the disease of chemical dependence have a *compulsion* to use alcohol/drugs. They have behavior and mood swings. Their drinking/using habits are *inappropriate, unpredictable, excessive,* and *constant.*

■ Chemical dependence is a *primary* disease. That means it isn't the result of some other disease or problem.

For a long time, doctors thought it was. They told their patients, "Let's find out what's *really* wrong with you and then you won't have to drink/use anymore." That didn't work. Chemical dependence isn't caused by other diseases. Instead, *it* causes *them.*

Chemical dependence leads to diseases of the liver, stomach, heart, and brain, to name just a few important organs. It also leads to mental and emotional problems like mood swings and memory loss.

I really do love my parents, I love them a lot — but I feel angry at them most of the time. And embarrassed by them some of the time. And even frightened by them . . . and let down. **Betrayed.**

I hate to admit this, but sometimes I even wish I was an orphan.

IMPORTANT

If you come from a place where people say bad things about alcoholics and drug addicts, you may be wondering if chemical dependence is really a disease after all. You may be wondering if what they're saying is true: that chemical dependence is a *moral issue*, and that chemically dependent people could change if they tried.

Please read these lines out loud:

> *chemical dependence is a disease*
>
> *chemical dependence is a disease*
>
> *chemical dependence is a disease*
>
> *chemical dependence is a disease*
>
> *chemical dependence is a disease*

It may take a while, but one day you'll believe them. And when you do, you'll start seeing your parents in a brand new light: as sick people who need help.

When I hear Mom or Dad talk on the phone and tell a friend how high they got last night, or apologize for something they said or did, or brag about how they told so-and-so where to get off, I pretend I'm not listening. Sometimes I even close my door and lay on my bed and put my pillow over my head to shut it out.

Myth:

Alcoholics/addicts are skid row bums — men who live in the streets and can't hold jobs.

Fact:

Most chemically dependent people have jobs. (Ninety-five percent of all alcoholics go to work every day.) Most chemically dependent people live with their families in respectable neighborhoods.

Some are men — but some are women. Some are adults — but some are teenagers. And some are children.

I heard my parents fighting last night, calling each other obscene names, saying foul things about each other. I heard my mother crying and my dad pleading and both of them screaming. They don't know how my gut twisted around in a little ball, squeezing tighter and tighter until I thought I'd puke.

WHAT HAPPENS TO PEOPLE WHO HAVE THE DISEASE OF CHEMICAL DEPENDENCE?

They always get worse unless they get help.

Once they develop the disease, they have it for the rest of their lives. That's because chemical dependence is a permanent disease.

People who have it can be treated. They can stop getting sicker *as long as they stop using alcohol/drugs.*

If they don't get help, they usually die prematurely — either as a direct result of the disease, or as the result of something else that can be traced back to the disease.

■ According to insurance company statistics, an alcoholic who keeps drinking has an average lifespan *12 years shorter* than the nonalcoholic.

■ Heavy drinkers are *three times* more likely to have fatal strokes than people who don't drink.

There are some things we never talk about around my house. Like the times my parents come in laughing, stumbling in the door, falling over chairs, noisily raiding the refrigerator, banging the coffeepot around. I never tell them that I lay there and listen and worry that one of them will forget to put out a cigarette and we'll all burn to death in our sleep.

I never tell them what I do when they're away. I'm supposed to go to bed, but I don't. I stay up watching TV until I hear their car pull in the garage. Why shouldn't I?

I never tell them about my friends coming over. I know they don't want me to run around with John because "he isn't very nice" (their opinion!). But what am I supposed to do, sit here by myself? I get so lonely. And if I tell them they just laugh at me and call me a baby, or get mad and tell me to shut up and grow up.

Myth:

Alcoholics/addicts are bad people. There is something wrong with them that makes them want to use alcohol/drugs.

Fact:

Alcoholics/addicts are just like other people, with one important exception: They can't use alcohol/drugs without somehow losing control of their lives.

They aren't bad people. They're *sick* people.

A couple of times when my parents have been out of the house, I've gone into the liquor cabinet and tried some of it myself. The first time I just poured a bunch into a glass and held my nose and swallowed it. It burned all the way down, and then in a while it felt kind of nice. Later that night I threw up, but they were both passed out in bed and didn't hear me (lucky for me!).

WHAT CAUSES THE DISEASE OF CHEMICAL DEPENDENCE?

No one knows for sure. But there are several theories that may help to explain it.

One theory says that chemical dependence may be hereditary. It does tend to run in families. And there's about a 25 percent chance that the child of one or more chemically dependent parents will become chemically dependent.

Other theories say that chemical dependence may be related to specific personality types.

What we *do* know is that all kinds of people become chemically dependent. Rich people. Poor people. People of all races and creeds. Professional people and working-class people and unemployed people. Husbands and wives. Fathers and mothers. Grandparents. Even children.

We also know that in order for the disease to be active, the chemically dependent person must use alcohol/drugs. For the disease to be arrested, the person must stop using all mood-changing substances.

I come home from school hungry and go to the fridge and what I find is a half-eaten jar of peanut butter, some moldy bread, and two sixpacks of beer. There's *always* beer in the house, so why can't there be something decent to eat?

It makes me angry and sad. Don't I deserve good food? Am I supposed to do the grocery shopping too? I do just about everything else around here.

Myth:

An alcoholic/addict is someone who drinks/uses every day.

Fact:

A person can drink or use other mood-altering drugs once a month, once a week, even a few times a year and still be chemically dependent.

It's not *how often* people drink/use that really matters. It's *what happens* to them and to others around them when they drink/use that makes the difference.

If the use of alcohol/drugs causes any continuing disruption in their personal, social, physical, spiritual, and/or economic life, *and they don't stop using*, then they are chemically dependent.

I get scared sitting home by myself all the time. Every little noise in the house sounds like an elephant in the next room. I go to the living room and turn on the TV, then I end up leaving the picture on and turning the sound way down so I'll be sure to hear if anyone tries to break in. Lately I've been keeping a knife under the pillow on the couch, just in case.

WHAT <u>DOESN'T</u> CAUSE THE DISEASE OF CHEMICAL DEPENDENCE?

We *do* know that chemical dependence *isn't* caused by any of these:

- lack of willpower

- "weakness of character"

- "immoral" or "sinful" behavior

- outside influences like an unhappy marriage, an unhappy childhood, trouble on the job, or peer pressure

*So how come Dad gets mad at **me** on nights when Mom goes out? Is it **my** fault? He sits in his chair pretending to read a magazine but what he's really doing is looking at his watch over and over again, and if I move or say a word he starts shouting **go do your homework** or **get to bed** or **don't you have anything constructive to do?** Once I tried talking to him — I mean, it bothers **me** too — and he yelled at me to mind my own business, that I was just a kid and should keep my nose out of it.*

Sometimes I hate both of them, and then I feel so misunderstood.

WHAT ELSE DEFINITELY <u>DOESN'T</u> CAUSE THE DISEASE OF CHEMICAL DEPENDENCE?

YOU.

If someone you know is alcohol/drug dependent, IT ISN'T YOUR FAULT.

Nothing you did caused it. Nothing you are doing keeps it going. Nothing you can do can make it go away.

It Has Nothing To Do With You.

No matter what your parents may say. No matter what you may think. No matter how you may feel.

You Are Not Responsible.

My birthday was the worst. My parents decided to do something really special — take me out to dinner at a fancy restaurant — and everything was fine for the first hour, but then they kept ordering drinks and getting more and more smashed. And there I sat getting more and more worried about the drive home.

Finally I worked up my courage and said, "Mom and Dad, please don't drink anymore tonight." I was so scared my voice shook.

At first they were surprised, then they were angry. Who was **I** to tell **them** what to do? My Dad asked for the check right away and we left without eating the dessert we ordered. All the way home I got accused of being ungrateful and spoiling the evening.

It wasn't **me** who got drunk. Although sometimes I wish I could.

Myth:

Someone who drinks/uses only a little alcohol/drugs can't be chemically dependent.

Fact:

It's not *how much* people drink/use that really matters.

It's *what happens* to them and to others around them when they drink/use that makes the difference.

Did you ever see a shy person turn into the life of the party? Did you ever see a nice person turn nasty or a happy person burst into tears for no reason? Did you ever see a quiet person turn into a mile-a-minute talker? These can all be possible signs of the disease of chemical dependence.

*I've tried talking to my Mom about my Dad's drinking. I know she's hurting — I can see it in her eyes and in the way she acts around him. All I want to do is help. But she won't even admit there's a problem. She keeps making excuses for him. **He's tired . . . he had a hard day at work . . . you don't know the pressure he's been under . . . you're too young to understand. . . .** What **really** gets to me is when she tells me I didn't see something when I know I did. I say, "Mom, he could barely walk last night," and she says, "That's not true, dear, your dad was perfectly fine."*

*Why does she keep covering up for him? And why does it make **me** feel stupid? And crazy?*

CAN THE DISEASE OF CHEMICAL DEPENDENCE BE CURED?

No.

But it CAN be arrested. With help, chemically dependent people can stop getting worse and start getting better.

Help might involve joining Alcoholics Anonymous (A.A.), Narcotics Anonymous (N.A.), or Cocaine Anonymous (C.A.). It might involve going into a treatment center or clinic. It might involve private counseling or therapy. It *always* involves being willing to stop using alcohol or other drugs.

The other day I decided to do something really nice for my Mom. I gathered up all the laundry and washed it and dried it and folded it and started putting it away. I open my Dad's sock drawer and I can't believe my eyes. There's this little glass bottle with this little spoon attached to it, and inside the bottle is this white stuff.

I've seen pictures of cocaine. I've heard about what it does to people — how it doesn't take much to get hooked on it.

*I've known for a long time that my parents smoke grass. All their friends do, too. That really bothers me, but this cocaine thing **scares** me. A lot.*

*People **die** from cocaine. Or go to jail, if they get caught.*

Am I supposed to just keep my mouth shut? Am I supposed to tell somebody? Does my Mom know? Does she do coke, too?

I wish I'd never found it. I wish I didn't have to think about any of this.

34

Myth:

An addict is someone who uses hard drugs, like cocaine or heroine or PCP. You can't be an addict if all you use is marijuana or downers or uppers.

Fact:

Marijuana, downers, and uppers are drugs. (By the way, so are caffeine and nicotine.) Therefore, people who use them can become addicted.

A Drug Is A Drug Is A Drug.

It's okay for **them** to call each other names or run each other down or tell me how mad they are at each other, but if I say anything, watch out! And if I **don't** say anything, watch out! Confusion City! Either I get accused of taking sides, or I get accused of **not** taking sides.

Whatever I say or do is wrong. Why don't they just leave me out of it?

Myth:

An alcoholic is someone who drinks hard liquor, like Scotch or whiskey or vodka or gin. You can't be an alcoholic if all you drink is beer or wine.

Fact:

Alcohol is a drug. Beer and wine contain alcohol. Therefore, people who drink beer and wine can be alcoholics.

A Drug Is A Drug Is A Drug.

I find bottles in the weirdest places. Under the car seat. Down in the basement behind my Dad's workbench. In shoeboxes in the hall closet. Once I even found one inside the toilet tank. I had flushed the toilet and it kept running and I opened the top to find out what was wrong, and there it was — one of those pocket-sized bottles of booze.

Whenever I find one I feel scared and disgusted and confused. I don't want to believe what I'm seeing. Sometimes I get mad enough to pour the stuff out, but the mad feeling doesn't last and pretty soon I feel guilty again.

I feel guilty almost all the time. Scared, disgusted, confused, and guilty. Mom and Dad think I'm a basically happy person, which goes to show how much they know. They know *zero* about how I feel inside.

CLUES TO THE PRESENCE
OF CHEMICAL DEPENDENCE

How can you tell if your parents are chemically dependent? Read through the following behavior "clues" and decide which sound true to you.

1. They drink/use more now than they used to.

2. They do things while they're drinking/using, and later they deny them or say they've forgotten them.

3. They refuse to talk about their drinking/using.

4. They make — and break — promises to control or stop their drinking/using.

5. They lie about their drinking/using.

6. Most of their friends are drinkers/users.

7. They make excuses for their drinking/using or try to justify it.

8. Their behavior changes when they're drinking/using.

9. They avoid social functions where alcohol isn't served and other drugs aren't available or permitted.

10. They sometimes drive while drunk or under the influence of other drugs.

11. Sometimes after a drinking/using episode, they apologize for the way they acted.

12. They hide alcohol/drugs around the house or in the car or garage.

Maybe it's my fault. Maybe if I were a better person this wouldn't be happening to my family. Maybe if I worked harder, prayed harder, tried to be nicer to my sister, studied more, kept my room clean, didn't talk back as much, or maybe if I was never even born — maybe then my Dad wouldn't have to drink.

MORE CLUES TO THE PRESENCE
OF CHEMICAL DEPENDENCE

Your parents' behaviors don't provide the *only* clues to the existence of chemical dependence. *Your own behaviors and feelings can also be revealing.* Read through the following and decide which sound familiar.

1. I'm afraid to be around them when they're drinking/using.

2. I'm suspicious of their promises.

3. I feel anxious and tense around them.

4. I don't trust them.

5. I feel embarrassed when they're drinking/using.

6. I feel guilty when they're drinking/using.

7. I lie about them to other people.

8. I hate holidays because those are times when they're almost certain to drink/use.

9. I make excuses for them.

10. I'm afraid to ride in the car with them when they've been drinking/using.

I have a hard time concentrating in school. I know my parents are having trouble. Nobody ever tells me anything, so I have to guess. Part of the trouble is money, but I'm really confused about it — one day they yell and scream at me that they can't afford something, then the next day they go out and buy something that costs even more, or they spend a ton of money at the liquor store.

I know how much that stuff costs. I've seen them come home with a hundred dollars worth of booze. They can't afford to buy me new running shoes, but they always have enough dough for whiskey and vodka and brandy.

So there I am, sitting in school, worrying about money but mostly worrying about **them**. And then my teacher says something smart, like "Daydreaming again?" or "Earth to Peter! Come in, Peter!"

HOW CAN YOU MAKE CHEMICALLY DEPENDENT PERSONS STOP USING ALCOHOL/DRUGS?

You can't.

You can pour their alcohol down the sink or flush their other drugs down the toilet, and it won't make any difference. They'll just get more.

You can nag and complain and cry and threaten, and it won't make any difference. They'll keep using until they get help — if that day ever comes.

You can be extra nice and take care of them and your brothers and sisters and the dog and the cat and the house and the yard, and it won't make any difference. In fact, it may make it *easier* for them to use alcohol/drugs because you'll be freeing them of so many of their responsibilities.

You can bribe them to stop using, and maybe they'll promise that they will. Maybe they'll even quit — for a while. Just to prove to you (and themselves) that they don't have a problem. But unless they get help staying stopped, they'll probably start using again sooner or later.

You didn't make your parents chemically dependent. You can't make them UN-chemically dependent. You can try, and you can keep trying for the rest of your life, but it won't work.

You can, however, take care of yourself. By admitting that the problem is real. By refusing to take the blame for it. And by refusing to cover up for it.

I feel really strange when they fight over me. Part of me feels guilty and ashamed, and part of me feels excited, even triumphant. Even if one of them hates me and the other one loves me, at least they know I'm alive. At least they're paying attention to me.

Then again, it might be better if I wasn't around. Then they wouldn't have anything to fight about and maybe they could start getting along again, and maybe Dad could stop drinking. Maybe.

STOP DENYING THE PROBLEM

If one or both of your parents is chemically dependent, now is the time to face the facts.

Something wonderful happens when you admit that the problem is real. *You start feeling less crazy.*

God, if you're listening, <u>don't</u> let my parents come drunk or high to the basketball game tonight. I want them to see me play so much . . . but not if they're drunk or high.

Maybe you could even keep them from going out drinking afterward, like they usually do, while I go home by myself.

God, it <u>hurts</u> if my parents show up drunk or high, and it <u>hurts</u> if they don't show up at all. Even though I try to pretend that I don't care.

STOP BLAMING YOURSELF
FOR THE PROBLEM

You didn't cause it, and you can't fix it. You didn't start it, and you can't stop it. IT ISN'T YOUR FAULT.

Even if your parents claim to drink or use because of you, *it isn't true.*

Something wonderful happens when you start believing this. The weight of the world falls off your shoulders. You feel freer. You feel untangled. You feel *happier.*

I wonder how long Randy's mom is going to let me keep crashing at their house. David's mom finally told me I couldn't do it anymore — **why don't you go home**, she said, **don't you have a home?** I've already lost some of my friends because their parents don't approve of me. I heard Randy's mom talking on the phone the other day, saying "Mike thinks he lives here or something, and if I wanted three kids I'd have three of my own. . . ." All I need is a place to sleep. An extra bed, a couch, a floor, anywhere quiet and away from my own house and all the fighting and bickering and bitching that goes on there all the time. When Randy's mom kicks me out, where will I go?

STOP TRYING TO COVER UP
THE PROBLEM

It may seem coldhearted and cruel, but *don't* clean up after your parents if they get sick after a bout of drinking/using. *Don't* lie for them to bosses and relatives. *Don't* try to hide their drugs or keep them away from places where they can get them. *Don't* be their parent.

Be responsible to them not for them.

I hate it when she does uppers. I can tell — she gets all jumpy and hyper and crazy. I end up fixing dinner for me and my brother and sister because *she* isn't hungry. I tiptoe around, trying to stay out of her way, because I know that when she starts coming down her good mood will turn into a bad mood. Unless she takes *more* speed, in which case she'll stay up all night and be a zombie in the morning.

I wish she could just sit still and *be* with us.

I thought people were supposed to get smarter as they got older.

WHEN THE GOING GETS ROUGH, GET GOING!

Living with chemically dependent parents can be a nightmare. Not *all* chemically dependent people are abusive, but some of them are. Here are some hard facts from the National Institute on Alcohol Abuse and Alcoholism's Fourth Report to Congress on Alcohol and Health:

- 60 percent of reported cases of child abuse involved alcohol

- 41 percent of reported cases of assault involved alcohol

- 39 percent of rapes involved alcohol

- 64 percent of criminal homicides involved alcohol

What can you do if your parents are abusive? Avoid getting into arguments with them. Don't let them trick you into fighting with them. Don't believe them when they call you names or say terrible things about you. And if it looks as though one of them could hurt you, LEAVE THE HOUSE AND CALL FOR HELP.

My whole life is a series of what ifs. Nothing is constant, nothing is consistent. Mom's rules are different from Dad's rules, and what they tell me to do today may not be true tomorrow. And something I do wrong today might be okay to do tomorrow.

One day they'll be really nice to me, then the next day they'll tell me I'm a rotten, spoiled, ungrateful kid. Sometimes when I do something they have a right to be angry about, they smile and pat me on the back and tell me to forget it, it's no big deal.

I don't know what I'm supposed to do. I don't know who I am. I don't know what I am. I don't know where I am. Sometimes I wonder if I'm going crazy.

YOUR PARENTS' CHEMICAL DEPENDENCE CAN MAKE <u>YOU</u> SICK

Chemical dependence acts like a *contagious* disease.

Even if you yourself don't use alcohol/drugs, just being around someone who is chemically dependent can make *you* sick.

Chemical dependence has been called a "family disease." That's because it affects everyone who lives with, loves, or works with the chemically dependent person. They can become *co-dependents*.

I remember when I was little how I used to spend hours and hours with a babysitter or sometimes my grandma. Lots of times I wouldn't see my Mom for a whole weekend. Sometimes she'd come and get me and take me into a bar with her if it was Sunday afternoon. Then she'd buy me all the pop and potato chips I wanted.

Or she'd leave me sitting in the car all by myself. "I'll only be gone a few minutes" was what she'd say, and I'd end up sitting there for hours and hours. And if I went inside to tell her I wanted to go home, she'd get mad. It was easier just to sit in the car.

CLUES TO THE PRESENCE
OF CO-DEPENDENCE

Are *you* a co-dependent? Following are some statements that describe the way co-dependents feel and act. See how many describe you.

■ Co-dependents often feel trapped, depressed, and alone.

■ Co-dependents feel embarrassed by the behavior of their chemically dependent family members — as if it reflects on *them*.

■ Co-dependents are easily hurt by what others say, feel, think, or do.

■ Co-dependents let others tell them how to feel, how to dress, and how to act.

■ Co-dependents work very hard to keep other people from being upset with them or disappointed in them. They may lie or distort the truth to avoid making others angry.

■ Co-dependents hide their less-than-perfect behaviors (like making mistakes, swearing, smoking, or overeating) from their family members.

■ Co-dependents are afraid to leave home for fear that something will happen to someone they love.

■ Co-dependents feel obligated to take care of other people. They feel guilty when they ask for something for themselves. They give up their own wants and wishes to make other people happy. On the other hand, they try to control other people in order to get what they want without having to come right out and ask for it. (If this sounds confusing and complicated, that's because it is!)

After my parents have had their drinks at night, I listen to them talk about the people they know, even our relatives. I hear them say what rotten, terrible, stupid, selfish, petty people they are. Then at other times I see them laughing with, drinking with, and putting their arms around these same rotten, terrible, stupid, selfish, petty people.

I don't get it. If they don't like them, why do they pretend to like them? What do they say about **me** when I'm not around? Are they just pretending to like me, too?

CO-DEPENDENT ROLES

Being co-dependent is hard work. It takes a lot of effort and energy to live with chemically dependent people! Co-dependents are clever, though. They come up with elaborate defenses just so they can make it through the day. These take the form of *roles* they play within their families.

Do any of these describe a role *you* play?

The Super-Responsible Kid. You're VERY organized. You take care of your brothers and sisters, clean the house, fix the meals, and do the laundry. Plus you do well in school. And inside you feel angry.

The Super-Flexible Kid. You go with the flow. Whatever happens, happens. If your parents promise to show up at your school play and don't, you shrug it off. If they tell you one thing in the morning and something else at night, you don't argue. You bend. And inside you feel angry.

The Clown. You see the funny side of everything. You're always good for a joke, a laugh, or a prank. Especially when things get tense at home. You make faces, act silly, and tell hilarious stories. And inside you feel angry.

The Peacemaker. You're always stepping into family fights and trying to stop them. You want everyone to feel better. You want everything to be okay all the time. And you tell yourself it's not nice to feel angry.

The Troublemaker. You're mad at your parents, and you'll show them! They can take their rules and stuff them! You talk back. You skip school. Maybe you even abuse alcohol/drugs yourself. Outside you're angry — and under all the anger is fear.

Sometimes I love my Dad so much I could burst. Sometimes I hate him so much I could shrivel up and die. Most of the time I try not to feel anything about him one way or the other. I try to mind my own business and be the best person I can be so he'll love me. But if he doesn't — I guess I'll have to learn to live with it. Who cares, anyway. No big deal.

CO-DEPENDENT BEHAVIORS
AND HOW TO CHANGE THEM

You can't make your parents less chemically dependent. *But you can make yourself less co-dependent.*

You can't change your parents' behaviors. *But you can change your own.* Starting with these:

Protecting Your Parents. You love them, so you lie for them, cover up for them, and make excuses for them. You even lie to your closest friends — and feel guilty and ashamed for doing it.

STOP IT. QUIT IT. CUT IT OUT. Let them experience the consequences of their own actions. By protecting them, you're making it easier for them to stay sick. (Which is NOT the same as MAKING them sick.)

Letting Them Decide How You Will Act And Feel. You get up in the morning and check out your parents before you decide if you'll have a good day. You plan your activities according to what you think *they* want and expect.

STOP IT. QUIT IT. CUT IT OUT. Start making your *own* decisions and living your *own* life.

I've tried talking to my Mom and Dad about drugs, but they don't listen at all. I try telling them it's dumb to use drugs. I try telling them they're ruining their health. Sometimes I even threaten them, saying I'm going to run away from home or kill myself or get even with them someday.

I want them to stop. I want them to stop NOW. What if they get caught? What if they get arrested or go to jail? I know they don't just **do** drugs, they also **sell** them to their friends. My parents are dealing!

So where am I supposed to go if they land in jail? Who's supposed to take care of me while they're locked up somewhere?

Plus I think what they're doing is **wrong**. Selling drugs is **wrong wrong _WRONG_**.

If I know about it and keep quiet, does that make me guilty, too? If I tell someone about it, does that make me a traitor to my own parents?

What if they went to jail because of me?

MORE CO-DEPENDENT BEHAVIORS AND HOW TO CHANGE THEM

Withdrawing From The Family And Avoiding Your Parents. You punish them with the silent treatment. You keep your thoughts and feelings to yourself. You stay so busy with school, sports, and work that you hardly have time to think or feel.

STOP IT. QUIT IT. CUT IT OUT. Treating your parents as if they don't exist won't help anyone, least of all you. They may be sick, but they're still human — and chances are they still love you *very much*. They just may not be very good at showing it. Don't cut them out of your life!

Blaming Your Parents For Everything That Goes Wrong In Your Life. You're angry and resentful, and you take it out on them. If you fail a test in school, it's their fault. If your boyfriend or girlfriend dumps you, it's their fault. If you cut your finger peeling potatoes, it's their fault. When you see them hurting or having problems, you feel good — it serves them right!

STOP IT. QUIT IT. CUT IT OUT. Again, your parents are people, and people have feelings. Try not to judge them so harshly.

He **promised** he wouldn't drink on the night of my party. My Mom helped me get the food ready, and my Dad fixed the speaker wire so the stereo sounded like a stereo again, and they got dressed up and greeted everyone at the door and for a while I thought everything was going to be okay. I even started to relax and have a good time. Then I went into the kitchen to make some more punch and opened the refrigerator and there was the martini pitcher, half empty, and I turned around and saw my Dad standing behind me looking guilty and stupid.

He couldn't give it up for just one night. Not even one night. Not even when he **promised** me.

Then he actually started dancing with my friends. He had his shoes off and was waving his arms around in the air and singing and making an ass of himself.

I wanted to die.

No wonder people left early. No wonder I didn't feel like going to school on Monday morning and facing everyone.

Dammit, he **promised**.

STILL MORE CO-DEPENDENT BEHAVIORS AND HOW TO CHANGE THEM

Feeling Ashamed And Covering It Up By Being Phony. You're ashamed of your parents. You're ashamed of your home. Maybe you don't even let your friends come over. You don't want anyone to know how ashamed you are, so you cover it up with a lot of bragging and showing off. Or you laugh and clown around to cover your shame. Or you shove other people around or do things to hurt them.

STOP IT. QUIT IT. CUT IT OUT. Covering up your shame is like getting on a giant merry-go-round. The more ashamed you feel, the more you try to cover it up; the more you cover it up, the more ashamed you feel. *Your parents are not you. You are not your parents.* Stand tall, be yourself, and be proud of who you are.

Joining Your Parents In Drinking/Using. You've heard the old saying, "If you can't beat 'em, join 'em." You can't "beat" your parents' problem, so why not try some alcohol/drugs yourself?

STOP IT. QUIT IT. CUT IT OUT. A large percentage of kids who come from chemically dependent homes become chemically dependent themselves, even though they swear that will never happen. *Don't set yourself up for a fall.*

I can't remember the last time I had a real conversation with my Mom. She sits in a chair staring at the television. Even when she isn't drinking she doesn't talk to me. It's like she doesn't even know I'm alive.

*I keep trying. I say, "Mom, I REALLY NEED to talk to you," but she just brushes me off and says **later** or doesn't say anything at all.*

Why am I even here? She obviously doesn't care about me. What difference would it make if I just left? She'd probably be glad if I went away and never came back.

What did I do to deserve the silent treatment?

Am I really so rotten that my own mother can't love me?

HEALTHY WAYS TO VENT YOUR ANGER

Admit it: you're REALLY ANGRY. Angry at your parents for being chemically dependent. Angry at them for making your life so miserable. Angry at them for not getting the help they need. Angry at them because you feel different, because your family is different and because you want to be like everyone else.

Let it out!

- Talk about your anger with someone you trust.

- Find yourself a punching bag, or a broomstick and a pillow. Give the pillow a few good whacks!

- Go out in the country and scream your head off.

- Start running or lifting weights.

- Dance until you drop.

Be mad at the right thing: the *disease*, not your parents, who are only its victims. Say to yourself, "It's hard to be angry at a disease, but I can do it. I've done lots of hard things in my life, and I can do this too."

I lay awake at night and wish they were dead. I imagine one or both of them getting killed in a car crash or hit by a train or falling off a bridge. Sometimes I think up ways to kill them and wonder how I can make it look like an accident. Then I stop myself and wonder how I could possibly think these things about my own parents.

What's wrong with me?

I must be sick.

SHARING THE SECRET

Chemical dependence is a disease of deception, denial, cover-ups, and lies. The longer it's kept secret, the worse it becomes, and the more cut off, isolated, and different you feel.

Find someone to talk to. Someone you trust. A minister or priest or rabbi, a teacher or counselor or friend or neighbor. DON'T FEEL GUILTY for sharing the secret. If your mom or dad had cancer, you'd talk about it, and you'd understand that it wasn't your fault. The same holds true for the disease of chemical dependence.

Give yourself permission to open up to someone who can listen and give you the support you need. You deserve it. You're worth it!

Whenever Dad gets high he starts out happy. He tells me what a great person I am and how proud he is of me and how glad he is that I'm his daughter. We have great conversations about life and the world, and I sit there like an idiot soaking up all that love and attention — and then, all at once, he gets ugly. Suddenly he's calling me names and telling me I'm worthless and saying awful things about my friends and accusing me of stuff I've never done.

It's happened a million times, but I'm never prepared. I always think that maybe this time will be different.

Maybe next time will be different.

THE POWER OF PRAYER

Pray for your family. Pray for your parents. Pray especially for the person you are angriest at — the one who has hurt you the most. Pray that God will help them find health and happiness.

It won't be easy. At first, it may be VERY difficult. The words may stick in your throat.

Keep trying. One thing you can be sure of: your parents *need* your prayers.

Mom and Dad don't drink all the time. Sometimes they stay sober for a week, a month, even three or six months at a time.

*But I can always tell when they're about to start drinking again. It hangs there like an invisible **something** in the air and I get a feeling of dread inside and sure enough, it's drinking time.*

I CAN'T STAND IT when they drink. I HATE IT when they drink.

I hate THEM when they drink.

I hate ME when I hate THEM.

THE HIGH COSTS OF
ALCOHOL/DRUG ABUSE

■ Each year, Americans spend $110 billion on drugs.

■ A report from the Bureau of National Affairs Inc., Washington, D.C.
says that on-the-job drug and alcohol abuse costs businesses nearly
$50 billion a year. This includes higher medical bills, insurance
premiums, business failures, and losses in productivity. Alcoholics
are absent more often and have more on-the-job accidents than
nonalcoholics.

■ The average monthly healthcare costs for families with an alcoholic
member is almost TWICE as high as for other families.

It's really ironic, all this talk about the "younger generation" and how "conservative" we are. About how we don't have any imagination and we don't believe in anything.

I believe in lots of things. I have opinions. I'd be glad to talk about them, too, if anyone cared enough to listen.

Come on, Mom and Dad. Ask me how I feel about politics, and the bomb, and drugs.

Just don't ask me when you're stoned.

THE DEADLY EXPERIMENT

In 1982, the National Institute on Drug Abuse estimated that 40 percent of all Americans between the ages of 18 and 25 had experimented with at least one illegal drug.

That figure is certainly higher today. How do we know? Because most of the major drug-producing nations are producing more illegal drugs than ever before. And more are being imported into the United States than ever before.

Someone is using them.

Probably someone you know.

My Dad got another DWI last night. Mom and I were at home when he called from the police station. Mom was frantic, but there was nothing she could do. He had to spend the night in jail.

I lay awake all night thinking about my Dad in jail, like some kind of criminal. I felt sorry for him — but I also felt kind of glad.

Last year a kid in my school got killed by a drunk driver. I kept thinking, **what if my Dad had been driving the car that killed her?**

What's wrong with him? Can't he see what he's doing? Doesn't he realize how dangerous it is to drive drunk? Doesn't he care?

Mom says he doesn't know when he's too drunk to drive. Sure. Right. I believe **that** *like I believe the moon is made of green cheese.*

He must know what he's doing. He just doesn't care. Does he?

The next time he gets a DWI, they take away his driver's license. Then he won't be able to drive at all.

I hope it happens soon.

THE GRISLY FACTS
ABOUT DRUNK DRIVING

■ More people are killed in car accidents in the United States every year than died in Vietnam, and approximately 60 percent of these deaths are related to alcohol or other drugs.

■ Every 20 minutes someone dies because of a drunk driver. That adds up to 30,000 deaths per year — or the equivalent of 2 fully loaded 747s crashing and killing everyone on board every week.

■ Most kids under age 15 who die in alcohol-related automobile crashes are passengers in vehicles whose drivers are under the influence.

■ Each year, 346 kids die and more than 12,000 are injured as passengers in cars where the drivers had been drinking.

■ Insurance companies estimate that 20 million drivers are problem drinkers.

■ 9,500 Americans under age 25 die each year in alcohol-related traffic deaths.

I can't stand it anymore. I can't stand the scenes and the arguments and the fighting. I can't stand the drinking and the yelling and the broken promises. I can't stand the silent treatment and the false affection and the boozy smelly hugs and the red eyes.

Yesterday I yelled back at my Mom. I said, "You should see yourself! You look like hell! And you stink!"

She slapped my face. Then she did it again. I guess I deserved it for mouthing off.

But I can't stand it anymore.

WHAT ARE WE DOING ABOUT DRUNK DRIVERS?

■ Experts estimate that 2/3 of all convicted drunk drivers are repeat offenders — people who have driven drunk before and will probably drive drunk again.

Clarence Busch, the driver who struck and killed 13-year-old Cari Lightner in 1980 (her mother went on to found MADD — Mothers Against Drunk Driving), had a long history of DUI (Driving Under the Influence) offenses, including three arrests, a license suspension, and an arrest for a hit-and-run — all *before* hitting Cari. After her death he was sentenced to two years in prison, was released in 18 months, got another driver's license, went in and out of jail again, obtained yet another driving permit, and ran a red light while drunk and hit a 19-year-old. That was his *sixth* offense for drunk driving.

The federal government and individual states are starting to crack down. Since 1982, more than 350 drunk-driving laws have been enacted. But we're still way behind other countries.

In Maine, for example, repeat offenders face less punishment than those convicted of shooting a moose out of season.

Two nights ago I thought I was going to die. My Dad picked me up after band practice as usual, and as soon as I got in the car I knew he was drunk. As usual. Then we got on the freeway and he couldn't stay in his lane, he was weaving back and forth across the road, and the next thing I knew this big semi was blaring its horn at us.

The sound filled the whole car.

Somehow my Dad yanked the wheel in the right direction. The semi passed us on the right, the driver still blaring his horn.

*We were going 65 miles per hour, and my Dad didn't even slow down. Instead, **he** laid on **his** horn and started swearing.*

I don't think he even realized what a close call it was.

Later I heard him telling Mom what happened. He made it sound like it was all the other guy's fault.

I'm scared to get in the car with him. Maybe I can get Maria's mom to drive me home from band practice from now on.

Maybe I should drop band practice. At least if I take the bus home from school I won't have to worry about my Dad getting us killed.

HOW OTHER COUNTRIES HANDLE DRUNK DRIVERS

■ In Australia, the names of convicted drunk drivers are published in local newspapers under the heading, "Drunk and in jail."

■ In South Africa, a drunk driver gets a 10-year prison term, a fine of $10,000, or both.

■ In Norway, a drunk driver is sentenced to three weeks in jail at hard labor and loses his or her license for a year. If he or she commits a second offense within five years, the license is revoked permanently.

■ In England, a drunk driver spends a year in jail, has his or her license suspended for one year, and pays a fine of $250.

■ In Russia, a drunk driver's license is revoked for life.

■ In Bulgaria, a second conviction of drunk driving carries a punishment of execution.

■ In El Salvador, drunk drivers are executed by a firing squad after their *first* offense.

Another wrecked Christmas. I hate holidays. Our family makes these plans like everything is going to be a big happy celebration. Buying presents, baking cookies, trimming the tree, all that crap.

Then comes the Christmas Eve party, when the relatives come by for dinner and Dad breaks out the first bottle of wine, and the second, and the third, and on and on until I lose count.

I know what's going to happen from then on. It's all so predictable. Everyone gets drunk, someone starts a fight, my big brother and I look at each other and leave the table and go upstairs and close our doors.

Here's what Christmas morning is like at our house: The dirty dishes are still on the table. The ashtrays are overflowing and stinky. Mom and Dad are hung over and grumpy. And my brother and I are supposed to open our presents and ooh and aah and pretend to be happy.

Guess what I want for Christmas next year. Two sober parents.

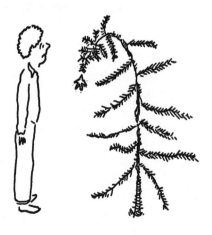

HOW YOU CAN MAKE A DIFFERENCE

■ Does your school have a chapter of SADD — Students Against Drunk Driving? If so, you may want to consider joining.

■ Refuse to climb into a car driven by a drunk or high adult — even if that adult is your parent. If possible, get your parent to leave the car where it is and take a taxi, or call a friend for a ride.

■ Find out about the drunk driving laws in your state. Find out about the drunk driving laws in other states. If you think a change is needed, write to your state representative or senator.

I learned at school that alcoholism is a disease. Sure it is. I never heard of a disease that forces someone to go to the liquor cabinet and take out a bottle and open it and start guzzling it.

I think I'll catch a few diseases of my own. Like the I-refuse-to-do-my-homework disease. Or I'll-never-pick-up-my-room-again disease. Or the I'm-not-going-to-do-the-dishes disease.

This whole disease thing sounds like a big excuse to me.

YOU'RE NOT THE ONLY ONE WHO HURTS

Chemically dependent people are people in pain. They may feel so much pain that they drink/use even more to numb themselves against it.

When your parents scream at you or call you names or read you the riot act, try to understand that they hurt. Try just listening quietly as they vent their anger and despair. Tell yourself, "I didn't cause this disease, I can't change it, I can't cure it."

I'm so ashamed of my parents. I'm ashamed of the way they look and the way they act and the way they drink. I'm ashamed of them for being alcoholics.

When people get sick, don't they try to get well? Don't they go to the doctor and get medicine? And if there's something that's making them sick, don't they try to stay away from it?

If my parents are sick with alcoholism, why don't they stay away from alcohol?

HOW TO GIVE YOUR PARENTS
WHAT THEY DESERVE

Your parents may give you a hard time. They may embarrass you. They may act stupid. They may run over your feelings until you wonder if you have any left.

But they're still your parents.

Treat them with respect and dignity — for your sake as well as theirs. Don't nag, argue, spy on them, dump their liquor or flush their drugs, scream at them or call them names. Think about the respect you give a close friend or teacher, then give the same to your parents.

Be accountable. Don't use your parents as an excuse to avoid your own responsibilities. Be on time, do your homework, be clean, keep your word, strive for honesty, and give yourself a pat on the back every time something goes even halfway right for you.

Why bother? Because you'll feel better about *yourself.*

I lied to my parents again today. Actually, I lied to them lots of times. It just seems easier to lie than to tell the truth.

I lied about where I went after school. I said I'd gone to Mandy's house when I really went to Jennifer's.

What's funny about it is, my Mom wouldn't care if I went to Jennifer's. She likes Jennifer.

So why did I lie about it?

Habit, I guess.

THE VALUE OF POSITIVE SELF-TALK

Children who grow up in chemically dependent families seldom get the love and support they need. Their parents simply aren't able to say the things their kids need to hear to feel good about themselves. Speaking through the pain of their disease, they say painful things. Hurtful things. Words that leave deep scars.

That's why you have to tell yourself the healing, positive things your parents may not be able to.

It will probably feel strange in the beginning, but give it a try. Stand in front of a mirror and practice saying these words to your own face:

"I am a lovable and capable person."

"I deserve the best from life."

"I am a special and unique person."

"It is all right to make mistakes."

"My parents really love me a lot, even if they don't know how to show it."

"I am not alone. There are lots of people in the same situation I'm in."

"I give myself permission to be happy."

"I'm okay. I'm okay. I'm okay."

Once you start believing your own words, some of your anger and frustration will subside. And you really *will* feel better about yourself.

I would like for five minutes to live in a house where people talk to each other and listen to each other and help each other solve problems and DON'T DO DRUGS.

Just five minutes. In a NORMAL house. It doesn't have to be like one of those always-happy-and-perfect-no-matter-what TV families. (I don't think they're so normal, either.)

But it does have to be a house where people DON'T DO DRUGS.

I wonder what it would be like.

COCAINE: NO LONGER COOL

People used to think that cocaine was cool, safer than heroin or PCP ("angel dust"), okay to use because rich and glamorous and famous people used it.

We know better now.

■ In 1986, Boston Celtics draftee Len Bias and Cleveland Browns safety Don Rogers both died of cocaine-related heart attacks. Bias had just signed a $1 million contract with the Celtics and a six-figure contract with the Reebok shoe company. Rogers was at a bachelor party on the night before he was to be married. Bias was 22, Rogers was 28. Their deaths occurred just eight days apart.

■ Between 1981 and 1985, the number of cocaine-related deaths in the United States *tripled.*

Heart attacks have been caused by as little as a single "line" of coke. *Users don't build up a tolerance.* A person can safely use a certain amount one day, then take the same amount the next day (or the next week, or the next month) and die.

Tonight my whole family went crazy.

It started when my Dad pulled his first beer out of the refrigerator. Mom starts ragging on him about it. *Don't drink that, you don't need that, why not go watch the news for a few minutes while I get dinner on the table.*

Just one, my Dad goes. *I had a hard day, I just want one, what's wrong with that?*

One turns into two, and two turns into three, and before you know it you're drunk, my Mom goes, her voice getting louder.

My Dad SLAMS the beer down on the counter and it sprays all over everything. Then he whacks my Mom.

My sister jumps up and starts shouting at him. He starts shouting at her. By now I'm crying and screaming. Dad grabs his coat and marches out the door and we hear his car screeching down the driveway.

Mom runs upstairs to the bedroom and slams the door and starts sobbing.

My sister and I stand there looking at each other. Then she runs out of the house.

I go upstairs and slam my door, too.

I'm not coming out.

PLAN FOR YOUR PERSONAL SAFETY

Know what's best for your own safety and *act on it*.

When your parents are drunk or stoned, don't argue with them or provoke them in any way.

Sometimes it's safest to say nothing. Sometimes it's safest to disappear. Sometimes it's safest to carry on as though everything is normal.

Only you can know what's right for you. Try never to put yourself in a situation where you might get hurt — and don't feel guilty because you're protecting yourself. Feel wise instead!

Planning for your personal safety isn't silly, nor is it a betrayal of your family. It's just good sense, and it will give you peace of mind — which you deserve.

For example: If one of your fears is that your parents will set the house on fire by passing out with a cigarette in hand, *be ready* in the awful event it ever happens. Locate the fire escapes. Make sure that your house has at least one smoke alarm, and that it's working. Plan for ways to alert others in the house. Then sleep soundly, knowing that you've done all you can do.

It's not easy to be practical about matters like these, but you're used to doing hard things. You do them all the time.

My parents kept saying, **Invite Jenny to dinner! We want to meet the new girlfriend!** *I kept coming up with excuses, and then I ran out, and I had to ask her over.*

I knew what would happen. The same thing that always happens. We all sat down to dinner and my parents proceeded to get drunk. Stoned. Intoxicated. Inebriated. Tight. Sotted. Soused. Loaded. Potted. Three sheets to the wind.

I know all the words. I looked them up a long time ago.

I really liked Jenny. But now I'm so embarrassed I don't think I can ever talk to her again.

Either I can't go out with anyone, or I have to sneak around.

Maybe I just won't have a girlfriend.

KNOW THE DIFFERENCE BETWEEN
SELFISHNESS AND SELF-PRESERVATION

One word that's often heard in chemically dependent families is *selfish*. People accuse one another of being selfish as if it were the most horrible thing imaginable.

To protect yourself from the craziness of living with chemically dependent parents, you need to understand the differences between *selfishness* and *self-preservation*.

■ **Selfishness** is getting your own way regardless of who gets hurt.

■ **Selfishness** is thinking only about your own pain and your own problems.

On the other hand,

■ **Self-preservation** is taking care of yourself and your health, refusing to be abused, saying NO to alcohol/drugs, and keeping quiet when that's the thing to do.

■ **Self-preservation** is insisting on doing something *you* like to do once in a while — something for *yourself*.

I keep the house picked up. I watch my little brother. I do the laundry and make sure dinner gets on the table. I mow the lawn. I answer the phone when it rings and give excuses why my parents can't talk. I answer the door when someone comes to our house and ask them politely to come back later, and when they come back I do it again.

I take care of everything. And I've stopped expecting anyone to take care of me.

Instead of crying and feeling sad, I just work harder.

Maybe if I do it long enough someone will start appreciating me.

TAKE TIME TO TAKE CARE OF YOURSELF

Living with chemically dependent parents can drain you physically, emotionally, and mentally. That's why it's important to stop and take stock every once in a while.

Check yourself out then and there. Are you safe? Are you warm? Have you had enough to eat? Are you afraid? What's happening at that moment in time? Is there anything you need to do right away to take care of yourself?

- Take it one day at a time. If that seems like too much, take it five minutes at a time.

- Try not to dwell on the past (which you can't change) or worry too much about the future (an unknown). Live in the moment. If you can, savor it!

- Look up the word *martyr* in the dictionary. Then decide not to be one!

I can't handle school anymore. What's the point? I go sit in class and read about stuff that doesn't have anything to do with ANYTHING, and learn a bunch of facts, and take a lot of stupid tests.

Besides, I can't think straight. Every day I sit in class reliving last night's fight around the dinner table. What if I hadn't said this, what if I had said that, what if I had just kept my mouth shut? Would Mom have stayed sober another hour or another ten minutes?

I always say or do the wrong thing.

So what if I flunk the math test tomorrow.

DETACHMENT: THE ART OF LETTING GO

Someday not too far from now, you won't be living with your parents anymore. You'll be away at school or off on your own somewhere.

What can you do to protect yourself until then?

You can begin to detach from their behaviors and their problems.

Start shifting your focus away from them and onto yourself. Start thinking about how their chemical dependence has affected you and what you can do about it. Start thinking about how you can heal yourself and go on to a fuller, freer, and healthier existence than your parents have been able to experience.

Detachment may sound like a cold and uncaring process. It isn't. It's the warm and life-affirming process of caring *for yourself.* It's an essential ingredient of any future happiness. It helps you to learn that you must work on your own problems and not blame others for your unhappiness; that you're responsible for your own behavior; and that the most helpful thing you can do for yourself *and your parents* is to put your own life in order.

I'm sick of hearing about what a perfect family I have. About what a perfect house we live in. About how lucky I am to have a Mom and Dad who let me go out as much as I want.

Nobody knows the truth. My parents don't **let** me go out. They just don't notice when I'm gone.

PRACTICING DETACHMENT

■ Make plans for yourself based on *your* needs. Start looking for things to do away from home.

What about taking an evening class? What about getting involved in an after-school club or activity? What about sports or studying with a friend — at his or her house, or the library?

■ Challenge yourself. The busier your brain and body are, the less time you'll have to worry and agonize over your home situation.

Sign up for a tough subject next quarter. Volunteer for something. Join a volleyball team or exercise class. Join 4-H. Learn to rollerskate.

■ For best results, balance your activities. Choose some physical, some mental, some work, some fun.

You can't change your parents, but you can still love them — which may get easier as you do it from a greater distance and a position of strength and self-confidence.

My parents are always telling me to be open and honest with them. If I have any questions, I'm supposed to ask them and not be afraid.

The trouble is, I know the questions I have are ones they don't want to hear. Like, if drugs are illegal and bad for you, why do you do them? And if alcohol should be "used in moderation," why do you get drunk so much?

My parents are always saying that if I'm curious about some drug, I should try it at home first. Right. I can just see my parents sitting there smiling while I smoke grass.

I tried some last week, but not at home. I was at Jerry's house and he pulled out a joint and lit it and passed it to me, and what could I do? Be a jerk and say no?

Nothing happened, anyway. Except I got a hu-MUN-gus headache and my throat hurt.

WARNING

Children of alcoholics/addicts have more problems with alcohol and other drug abuse than children from homes without chemically dependent family members.

Some sources estimate that from 40 to 60 percent of children of alcoholic parents become alcoholics themselves.

Half of all teenagers in America drink at least once a month. Nearly one out of every three high school students has alcohol problems.

Even grade-school children are getting hooked on mood-altering chemicals. The pressure is growing to try alcohol at earlier ages. One survey found that nearly 30 percent of fourth graders experience pressure to try alcohol. And alcohol use among sixth graders has more than doubled in recent years.

If you have never tried alcohol/drugs, DON'T. Learn to say no. Practice saying no. Mean it when you say it, and stick to it!

Four Ways To Say No:

1. "No."

2. "Nope."

3. "No thanks."

4. "I'm sorry, but I'm allergic to drugs. They make me break out in bad judgment."

YOUR WAY TO SAY NO (write it here):

"_____

_____

_____ "

All I ever wanted was a normal family. A family who had normal arguments and normal good times together and normal problems.

*I look around our house and everything **seems** normal. We have furniture just like other families. We have a dog and a cat. We have neighbors and a yard and a garden.*

So why am I always torn up inside? Why am I always angry and upset and edgy? Why am I failing in school? Why don't I have any friends?

There are eight million WHYS and no BECAUSES.

All I ever wanted was a normal family.

Is that too much to ask?

MOVING FORWARD

You may never have a "normal" family. Your parents may be actively chemically dependent for the rest of their lives. Even if they get help, they will still be special. They will need to keep working on their recovery for the rest of their lives.

Whether your parents get better or worse doesn't have to control *your* life, though. *You can learn to take care of yourself.* You can learn to live differently. Better. Happier. Chemically free.

Tell yourself this a dozen times a day or whenever you feel overwhelmed by your parents' behavior. It helps!

Even more important, *take action.*

There are places you can go to learn more about the disease of chemical dependence. Knowledge is your best and strongest defense.

There are people you can turn to for help. People who will be your allies and your friends.

You have already done something positive for yourself. You have read this book this far. Congratulations! That took time and courage.

Now you can do something else for yourself. You can read the last few pages. They're packed with names, addresses, telephone numbers, and titles — information you can use to take action and find out more.

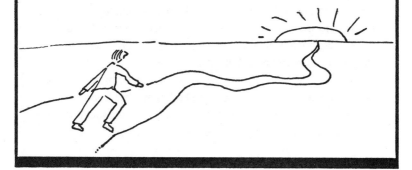

IF YOU KNOW THAT YOUR PARENTS ARE USING ILLEGAL DRUGS, SHOULD YOU TELL THE POLICE?

This topic has been in the news a lot, and we think it's worth considering here.

To be honest, we're not quite sure what to say. It's a sticky issue. The law is clear: illegal drugs are illegal drugs. But the facts and circumstances of people's lives aren't always as clear as the law.

At one extreme are kids whose parents are in deep with drugs and whose lives are in danger because of it. At the other extreme are kids whose parents use drugs very rarely and claim to use them responsibly. Somewhere in the middle are kids like Deanna Young.

One day in 1986, Deanna took her parents' marijuana, cocaine, and pills down to the police. She later said, "I thought the drugs would be taken away and that would be it."

But that wasn't it. First her parents were charged with possessing narcotics, and it looked as though they might go to jail for as long as three years. Deanna was placed in a shelter for abused children.

Their story seems to have had a happy ending. Instead of going to jail, Deanna's parents were allowed to enter a drug program. And Deanna moved out of the shelter and back home with her mother and father.

There have been several other cases of kids turning their parents in for drug use. Some had serious complaints — like the 13-year-old whose family had $10,000 worth of speed. But others seem to have decided that calling the police was a great way to "get even" with their parents.

We can't tell you what to do because we don't know what's happening in your family. But we can make this cautious recommendation: Talk to someone *anonymously* first. Check the phone book under "Crisis Intervention" and find a hotline number. Then dial it and tell the person on the other end what's been going on at your house. He or she should be able to give you some sensible advice.

You can also talk to a school counselor, but you probably can't do that anonymously. Depending on the circumstances, that person may be required by law to report what you tell him or her.

Naturally you don't want your parents using illegal drugs. But it's almost impossible to predict what will happen if you decide to report them. In some states you, like Deanna, may be placed in a shelter or a foster home. That may be a good thing, or it may not. You and your family may get a lot of attention from the news media, which is almost never a good thing. Solving personal problems gets harder when the problems go public.

There must be a better way, but no one seems to know exactly what it is — at least, not yet. *Your biggest concern should be your own personal safety.* If you feel that your safety is threatened, you should get out and get help, which will probably mean calling the police. If you feel that your safety is *not* threatened, we recommend that you start by getting advice anonymously, without putting your parents on the line — or in the lineup.

WHERE TO GO TO GET HELP

■ Look in the Yellow Pages under "Alcoholism" or "Alcoholism Information and Treatment Centers" and the White Pages under "Alcoholics" and "National Council on Alcoholism" and call each number listed there. Ask the persons on the other end how you can get information about chemical dependence.

■ Write to the National Office of Alcoholics Anonymous (A.A.), Box 459, Grand Central Station, New York, NY 10163 and ask for FREE literature on alcoholism.

■ Write or call Al-Anon Family Group Headquarters, Inc., PO Box 862, Mid-Town Station, New York, NY 10018. Telephone: (212) 302-7240. Tell them you need information on Alateen and would appreciate whatever FREE literature they can send you.

If it is at all possible for you to get to an Alateen group meeting, GO. It may be the best thing you ever do for yourself. In Alateen you'll learn how much love and support is available to you from other teenagers like yourself — all "different" like you.

Some parents are okay with their kids going to Alateen. Others aren't. Again, you're the best judge of your own situation, and only you know what to do. Go if you can; if you can't, find out about chemical dependence in other ways. Read everything about it you can get your hands on!

■ Write or call the National Association for Children of Alcoholics (NACoA) 31582 Coast Highway, Suite B, South Laguna, CA 92677. Telephone: (714) 499-3889. Ask for their reading list and other resources and a copy of their newsletter.

This nonprofit organization serves as a resource for anyone of any age who is the child of an alcoholic.

■ Write or call the Children of Alcoholics Foundation, Inc., PO Box 4185, Grand Central Station, New York, NY 10163. Telephone: (212) 351-2680. The Foundation publishes FREE reports on children of alcoholics.

■ Write or call the National Clearinghouse for Alcohol and Drug Information (NCADI), PO Box 2345, Rockville, MD 20852. Telephone: (301) 468-2600. Ask for reprints and brochures on alcoholism and chemical dependence. Some are free; some are available at a moderate cost.

The National Clearinghouse is the public information branch of the National Institute on Alcohol and Alcoholism.

■ Write or call the National Council on Alcoholism and Drug Dependence (NCADD), 12 West 21st Street, New York, NY 10010 and request information. Telephone: (212) 206-6770. Or check your telephone directory; NCADD may have a local affiliate you can call.

- If you need information *fast,* look in your telephone directory under Alcoholics Anonymous if *you* have a problem with drinking/using; Al-Anon if a family member has a problem with drinking; or Alateen if you are affected by a parent's, friend's, or relative's drinking problem. Alateen may not have a separate listing; if this is the case, call Al-Anon.

- Look around your school, neighborhood, and church or synagogue. Who is there for you to talk to? What about a counselor, a friend whose parents might understand, a youth group leader, a favorite teacher?

Sometimes an adult you want to talk to may be too busy with his or her own problems to be very helpful. Don't get discouraged. Go to the next one on your list, and then the next, until you find someone who will listen. Tell yourself "I'm special," "I deserve this," then go after what you need.

TO FIND OUT MORE

Several publications on chemical dependence are available from the Johnson Institute.

Alcoholism: A Treatable Disease. A straightforward look at the disease of chemical dependence, the confusion and delusion that accompany it, and the process of intervention. 25 pages.

Intervention: How To Help Someone Who Doesn't Want Help: A Step-By-Step Guide for Families and Friends of Chemically Dependent Persons by Vernon E. Johnson. The first book to describe the intervention process in terms that anyone can understand, it also tells how chemical dependence affects everyone around the sick person. 116 pages.

Can I Handle Alcohol/Drugs? A Self-Assessment Guide for Youth by David Zarek and James Sipe. Find out how chemicals might be affecting you in different areas of your life. Non-threatening, non-preachy, non-embarrassing. 32 pages.

Why Haven't I Been Able To Help? A look at co-dependent behaviors. 20 pages.

How It Feels To Be Chemically Dependent by Evelyn Leite. For recovering persons, chemically dependent persons, friends and loved ones who want to know more about the emotional effects of chemical dependence. 24 pages.

Chemical Dependence: Yes, You Can Do Something. The basic knowledge families need to help their loved ones *now*. Covers the disease concept, denial, delusion, how the family is affected, in easy-to-read, non-clinical language. 27 pages.

Chemical Dependence and Recovery: A Family Affair. Focuses on the family involved with chemical dependence. Topics include the disease and its phases within the family, the feelings of family members, and co-dependence. 39 pages.

Detachment: The Art of Letting Go While Living with an Alcoholic by Evelyn Leite. Some answers to hard questions for those who share their lives with an alcoholic/drug dependent. A good booklet for anyone trying to "let go." 30 pages.

To order, write or call:
Johnson Institute
7151 Metro Boulevard
Minneapolis, MN 55439-2122
In the United States: 800-231-5165
In Canada: 800-447-6660
In Minnesota: 800-247-0484 or 612-944-0511

When ordering, request a copy of the Johnson Institute catalog to find out about other publications.

YOU HAVE RIGHTS!

YOU HAVE THE RIGHT to be yourself and like who you are.

YOU HAVE THE RIGHT to refuse requests without feeling selfish or guilty.

YOU HAVE THE RIGHT to be competent and proud of your accomplishments.

YOU HAVE THE RIGHT to feel and express anger.

YOU HAVE THE RIGHT to ask for affection and help.

YOU HAVE THE RIGHT to be respected as a human being with feelings.

YOU HAVE THE RIGHT to be illogical in making decisions.

YOU HAVE THE RIGHT to make mistakes — and be responsible for them.

YOU HAVE THE RIGHT to change your mind.

YOU HAVE THE RIGHT to say, "I don't know!"

YOU HAVE THE RIGHT to say, "I don't agree!"

YOU HAVE THE RIGHT to say, "I don't understand!"

YOU HAVE THE RIGHT to say, "I want more!"

YOU HAVE THE RIGHT to offer no reasons or excuses for anyone else's behavior.

YOU HAVE THE RIGHT to have your opinions respected.

YOU HAVE THE RIGHT to have your needs be as important as other people's.

YOU HAVE THE RIGHT to be listened to AND understood.

YOU HAVE THE RIGHT to take pride in your body and define attractiveness in your own terms.

YOU HAVE THE RIGHT to grow, learn, change, and value your own experience.

And sometimes to make demands on others. . . .

Don't hide behind a wall of silence; it will destroy you. Know that you don't have to talk about your parents to anyone if you don't want to — only about yourself and your own dreams.

Inside you is a spark that tells you when something feels right or wrong. Watch for that spark, nurture it, trust it. It's your God's center, and it will protect you.

E.L.

P.L.E.

When the Johnson Institute first opened its doors in 1966, few people knew or believed that alcoholism was a disease. Fewer still thought that anything could be done to help the alcoholic or other drug dependent person except to wait for him or her to "hit bottom" and then pick up the pieces.

We've spent over twenty-five years spreading the good news that chemical dependence is a *treatable* disease. Through our publications, films, videocassettes and audiocassettes, and our training and consultation services, we've given hope and help to hundreds of thousands of people across the country and around the world. The intervention and treatment methods we've pioneered have saved lives, healed relationships, and brought families back together.

Today, the Johnson Institute is an internationally recognized leader in the field of chemical dependence intervention, treatment, and recovery. Individuals, organizations, and businesses, large and small, rely on us to provide them with the tools they need. Schools, universities, hospitals, and treatment centers look to us for experience, expertise, innovation, and results. We will continue to reach out to chemically dependent persons, their families, and the professionals who serve them . . . with care, compassion, and commitment.

JOHNSON INSTITUTE®

7151 Metro Boulevard
Minneapolis, MN 55439-2122

In the United States: 800-231-5165
In Canada: 800-447-6660
In Minnesota: 800-247-0484 or 612-944-0511